Sacred Mirror: The Power of Self-Love, Divine Union & Soul Connection

By Joy Hafner
TrueJoy Publishing

Copyright Page

Sacred Mirror: The Power of Self-Love, Divine Union & Soul Connection
© 2026 by Joy Hafner

This book is published by:
TrueJoy Publishing

Author: Joy Hafner
Publisher: TrueJoy Publishing

ISBN: 978-1-971164-77-9
ISBN: 978-1-971164-99-1

Cover design by TrueJoy Publishing
Interior design by TrueJoy Publishing

Printed in the United States of America

First Edition

Disclaimer

This book is intended for educational and inspirational purposes only. It is not a substitute for professional medical, psychological, legal, or therapeutic advice. The author shares personal experiences and spiritual perspectives that may not reflect every reader's path. Readers are encouraged to exercise discernment and seek qualified support when needed.

The concepts of "twin flames," "soulmates," and "soul family" are explored within a spiritual and symbolic framework. They are not presented as psychological diagnoses or guarantees of relational outcomes.

The author and publisher assume no responsibility for any loss, injury, or damage resulting from the use of information contained in this book.

Dedication

To the lovers who have seen themselves reflected in another's eyes—
to those who have felt the ache of separation,
and the joy of reunion within their own heart.

May you remember:
Love was never lost.
It was always you.

Epigraph Page

"Your twin flame is not found in another.
It is awakened in you."
— Joy

Author's Note

Why I Wrote This

There was a time when I believed love was something I had to find.

I believed in signs.
In destiny.
In the idea that if something was meant to be, it would reveal itself through intensity.

I believed that if a connection felt powerful enough, it must be sacred.

And like many who walk the path often described as the twin flame journey, I mistook activation for alignment.

I have loved deeply.
I have lost painfully.
I have chased.
I have been chased.
I have waited.
And eventually, I have let go.

For a long time, I believed someone else held the missing piece of me.

What I learned — slowly, and with humility — is that love was never missing.

It was simply waiting to be recognized in a different way.

The connections that once felt like destiny were not there to complete me.
They were there to reflect me.

What I once believed was another soul holding my answers was, in truth, a mirror — a sacred one.

A mirror that revealed my wounds.
My patterns.
My longing.
My projections.
My capacity to love.
And ultimately, my capacity to become whole.

This is what I now understand as the sacred mirror.

The people who enter our lives with extraordinary intensity are not always meant to remain. But they often arrive at pivotal moments, reflecting the parts of ourselves that are ready to be seen, healed, and reclaimed.

The journey many call the twin flame path did not give me a partner.
It gave me awareness.

It dismantled my illusions about romance.
It exposed my attachment wounds.
It asked me to confront abandonment, self-worth, fantasy, and fear.

It burned through the version of me who believed intensity meant destiny.

And what remained was something quieter.

Stronger.
Clearer.
More grounded.

I wrote this book not to romanticize spiritual relationships, but to bring clarity to them.

Because too many people are suffering inside spiritual language.

Too many are excusing chaos as divine timing.
Too many are enduring instability in the name of soul contracts.
Too many are waiting for reunion instead of embodying wholeness.

This book is not about finding "the one."

It is about recognizing what love is trying to show you.

It is about understanding love as frequency.
Love as responsibility.
Love as nervous system regulation.
Love as divine embodiment.

Most of all, it is about learning to stand in front of the sacred mirror of life and recognize the truth reflected there:

You were never incomplete.

You were always becoming.

I do not write these pages as someone who has mastered love.

I write them as someone who has been refined by it.

If these words bring you clarity, peace, grounding, or even the gentle dissolving of old illusions, then they have served their purpose.

You were never meant to chase the fire.

You were meant to become the light reflected within it.

With reverence and truth,
Joy

How to Use This Book

A Choose-Your-Own-Path Guide

This book is not meant to be read in only one way.

Love itself is rarely linear.

You may be arriving to these pages from many different places in life:

- In heartbreak
- In separation
- In confusion
- In partnership
- In healing
- Or in peaceful singleness

Each place calls for something different. Rather than forcing a single path, this book allows you to begin where your heart needs support most. Let the following guide help you navigate.

If You Are Healing from Heartbreak

Begin with:

Part I — The Mirror Within

Chapter 1 — *The Myth & Mystery of Twin Flames*
Chapter 2 — *The Runner & the Chaser*
Chapter 4 — *Self-Love as the First Sacred Union*
Chapter 9 — *The Reunion Within*

Move slowly.

Allow the reflections to reveal what the relationship activated within you. This stage is not about understanding the other person. It is about understanding what the connection mirrored. Your work is not to restore the relationship. Your work is to restore your stability.

If You Are in an Intense or Unclear Connection

Focus on:

Chapter 2 — *The Runner & the Chaser*
Chapter 5 — *Attachment vs Alignment*
Chapter 7 — *Discernment in Love*
Chapter 8 — *Sacred Reciprocity*

Ask honest questions.

Does this connection help you grow or does it destabilize you?

Are you calm and grounded, or reactive and anxious?

Are you expanding into yourself, or shrinking to keep the connection?

Intensity alone is not evidence of destiny.

Healthy love supports the nervous system, not overwhelms it.

If You Are in Partnership

Explore:

Chapter 8 — *Sacred Reciprocity*
Chapter 11 — *Sacred Union & Shared Purpose*
Chapter 12 — *Rituals for Conscious Relationships*

Love deepens through presence, responsibility, and emotional maturity.

Partnership is not sustained by chemistry alone.

It is built through communication, integrity, and shared growth.

Sacred love is not only felt.

It is practiced.

If You Are Seeking Closure

Begin with:

Chapter 9 — *The Reunion Within*

Then continue into:

Part III — Love Beyond Romance

Closure rarely comes from explanation.

It comes from integration.

As your nervous system settles and your perspective widens, the meaning of the connection becomes clearer.

Read until you feel your body soften.

That softness is often the first sign that healing has begun.

If You Are Single and Grounded

Read the book from beginning to end as refinement.

This path is not about finding someone.

It is about becoming someone who is aligned with secure love.

When you understand attachment, discernment, reciprocity, and emotional maturity, your relationships naturally reflect those qualities.

Secure love meets secure people.

You are not behind.

You are preparing.

A Final Note

This book is not here to tell you who your twin flame is.

It is here to help you recognize the sacred mirror present in every meaningful connection.

Every relationship has the potential to reveal something about your heart, your patterns, and your capacity to love.

The goal is not to chase intensity.

The goal is to become someone who can hold love with clarity, stability, and truth.

Begin where you are.

The mirror will meet you there.

Foundational Continuity Statement

Throughout this book, the following truths remain constant:

God is Love.
The Universe is Love in motion.
We are expressions of that Love.

Love functions as frequency, not possession.
Relationships are mirrors, not sources.
Union is a state of being, not an outcome.

These principles anchor every chapter.

If you feel confused at any point, return here.

Love is not external.

It is embodied.

The Sacred Mirror Path Map

The Phases & What They Teach

Powerful relationships often follow recognizable emotional patterns.

Not because destiny dictates them,
but because human psychology, attachment, and awakening move through cycles
of reflection.

When a connection acts as a sacred mirror, it reveals both our deepest capacity for
love and the places within us that still need healing.

These phases are not rigid rules.

Some people move through them quickly.
Others circle them more than once.

What matters is not the timeline —
but what each stage invites you to learn.

Phase 1 — Recognition

The connection feels immediate.

There may be a strong sense of familiarity, intensity, or emotional depth that is
difficult to explain.

Something about the interaction feels meaningful.

You feel seen.
You feel stirred.
You feel awake.

Teaching:
You are capable of profound emotional connection.

Shadow:
Projection — believing the other person carries qualities that are actually
awakening within you.

Phase 2 — Activation

The relationship accelerates.

Chemistry deepens.
Emotional vulnerability increases.
Personal histories begin to surface.

At the same time, old attachment patterns may begin to activate.

What once felt exhilarating may begin to feel destabilizing.

Teaching:
Your nervous system and attachment patterns are part of how you experience love.

Shadow:
Attachment — mistaking intensity for compatibility.

Phase 3 — Distance or Separation

The connection becomes complicated.

One person may pull away.
Communication may change.
Confusion often enters the dynamic.

This phase can feel painful, but it often exposes the emotional habits each person
brings into relationship.

Teaching:
Sovereignty — learning to stabilize yourself rather than relying on another person
to regulate your emotional state.

Shadow:
Obsession — attempting to control, chase, or explain the connection instead of
healing what it revealed.

Phase 4 — Turning Inward

At some point, the cycle of emotional reactivity becomes exhausting.

Instead of focusing on the other person, attention begins to shift inward.

You begin rebuilding your sense of self.

Boundaries strengthen.
Clarity grows.
Self-respect returns.

Teaching:
Self-love and emotional responsibility.

Shadow:
Spiritual bypassing — pretending the work is finished instead of continuing to grow.

Phase 5 — The Internal Reunion

Something quiet begins to settle.

You no longer need the relationship to resolve in a particular way.

Your nervous system becomes calmer.

Your sense of identity no longer depends on the connection.

Peace arrives — not because circumstances changed, but because your relationship with yourself did.

Teaching:
Wholeness.

Shadow:
Subtle ego inflation — believing awakening makes you superior rather than simply more aware.

The Deeper Purpose

The sacred mirror is not about perfect romance.

It is about reflection.

Some relationships remain in our lives.
Others serve as catalysts and then fade.

Either way, the real reunion is not between two people.

It is the moment when you recognize the stability, clarity, and love that were always available within you.

And from that place, every relationship you build moving forward becomes healthier, calmer, and more conscious.

A Note on Discernment & Safety in Love

This section matters.

Spiritual language should never override personal safety. Intensity does not equal compatibility. Chemistry does not equal alignment. Twin flame language should never:

• Justify emotional abuse
• Excuse inconsistency
• Minimize red flags
• Replace accountability
• Encourage waiting in dysfunction

Love that is divine will not destabilize your nervous system chronically.

Sacred love does not:

Gaslight.
Control.
Isolate.
Threaten abandonment.
Demean.

If you feel smaller, fearful, confused, or unsafe —
pause.

No spiritual explanation redeems mistreatment. Discernment is not cynicism.

It is maturity.

The most sacred relationship you will ever have
is the one with yourself.

Protect it.

Honor it.

Strengthen it.

Love is not proven by suffering. It is revealed through stability.

Table of Contents

PART I — THE MIRROR WITHIN
Awakening Through Reflection

Chapter 1

The Myth & Mystery of Twin Flames
Where Recognition Becomes Remembrance

The Story We Were Told

There is an ancient story that human beings once walked the earth whole.

Plato wrote
of souls split in two, wandering in longing.
Eastern mystics spoke of divine counterparts meeting across lifetimes.
Modern spirituality romanticized the idea into destiny — one person, one soul, one flame meant only for you.

It is a beautiful story.

And like all powerful myths, it holds a truth but not the truth most people think. Because the twin flame is not your missing half. It is your mirror. And mirrors do not complete you. They reveal you.

The First Time I Felt It

The first time I experienced what people call "twin flame energy," it did not feel calm. It felt electric. It felt like my nervous system had been struck by lightning. Like something ancient inside my body recognized something before my mind could make sense of it. The eye contact was too long. The silence too loud. The air too charged.

It was not just attraction. It was activation. But here's what I didn't understand then: Activation does not mean alignment. Recognition does not mean readiness. Intensity does not mean destiny. At the time, I mistook the shock for certainty. Now I understand something deeper. The body can recognize familiarity even when that familiarity is unfinished pain.

What Is Actually Happening in the Body

When someone feels like a twin flame, several systems activate at once:
- Attachment wiring
- Trauma memory
- Dopamine reward cycles
- Mirror neuron resonance
- Spiritual archetypal projection

It feels cosmic.

But often, it is also neurological. When the nervous system detects someone who mirrors our deepest wounds and our highest potential at the same time, it reacts as if something monumental is happening.

Because it is. But not always in the way we imagine. The twin flame experience is less about "finding your other half" and more about your psyche recognizing: There is something in this person that reflects unfinished integration within me.

That reflection can feel divine. It can also feel destabilizing. Both can be true.

Twin Flames as Catalysts, Not Completion

The most dangerous misunderstanding of twin flame mythology is this:
"If I just stay, endure, chase, or prove myself, we will unite, and everything will finally make sense."
But the twin flame journey is not designed to reward endurance. It is designed to initiate growth.

Twin flame energy surfaces:
- Abandonment wounds
- Control patterns
- Fear of engulfment
- Over giving tendencies
- Identity collapse inside relationships

It magnifies both shadow and light. If both individuals are emotionally mature and regulated, this amplification becomes creative fire. If either is unhealed, the amplification becomes combustion. Healed love builds worlds. Unhealed love burns them down.

Divine Frequency vs Trauma Chemistry

There is something sacred about deep recognition. But not everything that feels sacred is healthy. Trauma bonding can feel spiritual. Intermittent reinforcement can feel fated. Unavailability can feel mysterious.

The empath often feels magnetized toward the avoidant because chaos feels familiar. The wounded child inside us sometimes mistakes unpredictability for passion.

Twin flame mythology becomes dangerous when it encourages people to ignore:
- Inconsistency
- Emotional unavailability
- Disrespect
- Boundary violations
- Manipulation disguised as destiny

Love is frequency. But frequency must be stable to be sustainable. If love destabilizes your nervous system chronically, that is not divine union. That is dysregulation.

The Mirror Concept (The Real Meaning)

A mirror does three things:
1. It reflects what is present.
2. It does not judge what it reflects.
3. It cannot change what stands before it.

Twin flame energy reveals:
- Where you abandon yourself
- Where you overextend
- Where you collapse boundaries
- Where you seek validation
- Where you fear being fully seen

The person becomes the mirror. But the work is always yours. When we chase the mirror instead of integrating what it reveals, we remain stuck in longing.
When we turn inward and ask, "What part of me is this connection awakening?"
— the journey transforms.

The twin flame is not the prize. Awakening is.

The Inner Masculine & Feminine

Within each person lives polarity:

The inner feminine — receptivity, emotion, intuition, creativity.

The inner masculine — protection, structure, discernment, boundaries.

When these energies are fractured internally, we unconsciously seek someone externally to compensate. The over-functioning feminine seeks containment. The rigid masculine seeks softness.

The anxious seeks reassurance.
The avoidant seeks distance.

But when inner polarity harmonizes:
You stop chasing intensity.
You start valuing stability.
You choose presence over possession.
Self-love becomes the first sacred union. Without it, no external union can remain grounded.

Cautionary Wisdom: The Healed & The Unhealed

There is a painful pattern that repeats often in spiritual communities: The healed, self-aware person meets someone charismatic but unintegrated. The chemistry feels cosmic.

The red flags are rationalized as growth edges. The wounds are framed as destiny. The imbalance is endured in the name of awakening.

But healed falling for unhealed without discernment does not create sacred union. It creates spiritualized self-abandonment.

Divine love does not require you to tolerate chaos. Divine love is clean. Grounded. Respectful. Reciprocal.

If the connection requires you to shrink, chase, or destabilize yourself to keep it — it is not sacred union. It is unfinished work. And unfinished work can still be holy — if you turn inward instead of clinging outward.

The Real Twin Flame

The deepest truth?
The twin flame journey ends where it begins. Within.
When your inner masculine protects your inner feminine. When your heart trusts your boundaries. When your nervous system feels safe without external validation. When you no longer crave possession — only presence.
Then love changes. You stop searching for someone to complete you. You begin attracting people who reflect your coherence. A twin flame is not found. It is recognized. And then remembered within.

TrueJoy Alchemy Pause

Place one hand over your heart.
One hand over your lower belly.
Breathe slowly.
Ask yourself:
What in me was activated by my last intense connection?
Where did I abandon myself?
Where did I grow?
Sit with the answers without judgment.
Mirrors are teachers.

Ritual: Mirror of the Soul

Sit before a mirror. Light a candle.
Gaze into your own eyes.

Whisper:
"I am the love I have been seeking."
Place one hand on your heart.
One on your belly.
Visualize a steady golden flame at your center.
Not flickering.
Not frantic.
Not desperate.
Steady.
This is your true twin flame.
Repeat for seven days.
Notice the difference between longing and belonging.

Reflection Prompts

- When has intensity confused me into believing something was destiny?
- What does healthy love feel like in my nervous system?
- Where do I still seek validation outside myself?
- What would it mean to choose peace over passion?

Closing Mantra

May my love be steady as flame,
pure enough to warm the world,
wise enough not to burn it.

Chapter 2

The Runner & The Chaser

The Dance of Separation, Surrender, and Nervous System Awakening

When Love Turns Into Fear

After recognition comes activation. After activation comes expansion. And almost inevitably — comes disruption.

The twin flame narrative often romanticizes reunion. But what most people experience first is separation.

One leans in.
One pulls away.

One reaches.
One retreats.

And both are confused.

When I first experienced this dynamic, I thought something had gone wrong. We had felt so aligned. So certain. So electric.

How could something that felt divinely orchestrated suddenly feel destabilized?

The answer was simple — and brutal.

Because intensity had activated what wasn't healed.

The Sacred Polarity (What's Really Happening)

The runner–chaser dynamic is not a spiritual punishment. It is attachment activation. When two people connect at high emotional depth, their nervous systems begin scanning for threat.

The anxious-leaning nervous system feels:

"If this leaves, I will collapse."

The avoidant-leaning nervous system feels:

"If this gets too close, I will disappear."

Neither person is wrong.

Both are protecting something old.

The runner protects autonomy.
The chaser protects connection.

But beneath both is fear.

Fear of abandonment.
Fear of engulfment.
Fear of being unworthy.
Fear of being seen too clearly.

This is why the dynamic feels cosmic. Because it is childhood wiring meeting adult intimacy.

The Chaser: When Love Feels Like Survival

Chasers are often heart-led, intuitive, deeply feeling individuals. They sense the sacredness of the bond. They see potential. They feel connection in their bones.

But when distance appears, their body shifts into pursuit.

Texts become more frequent.
Explanations become longer.
Reassurance becomes necessary.

The thought pattern sounds like:

"If I just love harder, they'll stay."
"If I can prove I'm safe, they'll open."
"If I don't reach, I'll lose them."

But chasing is not devotion.

Chasing is fear seeking regulation through another person. And it never works long-term. Because no one can regulate your nervous system for you consistently. That is work you must learn internally.

The Runner: When Love Feels Like Threat

Runners are often misunderstood.

They are not always cold.
They are not always manipulative.
They are often overwhelmed.

Deep intimacy feels exposing. Being seen too clearly feels dangerous. If they grew up in environments where vulnerability was punished, criticized, or ignored, love can feel like loss of control.

So, they create distance. Not because they don't care. But because their body associates depth with danger.

The internal dialogue sounds like:

"This is too much."
"I'm losing myself."
"I can't meet these expectations."
"I'm not enough."

Withdrawal becomes protection. Silence becomes control. Distance becomes relief. But avoidance does not create peace. It creates fragmentation.

The Energetic Illusion

Here's where spirituality complicates things. Because when two people share high chemistry and deep emotional mirroring, the pull doesn't disappear with separation. It lingers. It feels psychic. Synchronic. Unfinished.

But intensity does not mean incompatibility has vanished. It means unresolved attachment still exists. And until both people regulate internally, reunion simply recreates the same cycle.

Many twin flame journeys stall here. Because neither person understands that the separation phase is not about the other. It is about self-regulation.

The Moment Everything Shifted

I remember the exact moment I stopped chasing. It wasn't dramatic. It wasn't empowering at first. It felt like exhaustion.

I realized I was trying to hold together something that required two stable nervous systems — not one hyper-functioning one. And I asked myself something I had avoided:

"If this connection disappeared entirely… who would I be?"

The answer terrified me. Because I had wrapped identity, worth, and spiritual narrative around the connection.

That is when I understood:

I wasn't chasing love. I was chasing certainty. And certainty cannot be extracted from another person. It must be cultivated within.

Surrender Is Not Giving Up

Surrender in twin flame mythology often gets misinterpreted. It does not mean tolerating disrespect. It does not mean waiting passively. It does not mean suppressing emotion. It means releasing control over outcome.

It means saying:

"I will not abandon myself to keep this connection alive."

When the chaser stops chasing, two things happen:

1. They regulate.

2. The dynamic changes.

Sometimes the runner returns.
Sometimes they don't.

But either way, the chaser regains sovereignty. And sovereignty is the real initiation.

What Happens When Roles Reverse

Many twin flame journeys include role reversal. Once the anxious partner stabilizes, the avoidant partner may feel the energetic shift. The absence feels louder.

The space feels heavier. The nervous system that once sought distance now seeks reconnection. This is not karma. It is regulation.

When one person stops pursuing, the other feels the imbalance. But healthy reunion does not happen because someone misses you. It happens because both individuals are stable. If reunion requires one person to overextend again, the cycle restarts.

Alignment feels calm. Attachment feels urgent. Learn the difference.

The Gift of Separation

Separation serves several sacred purposes:

- It forces identity reconstruction.

- It exposes dependency.

- It reveals where self-worth was outsourced.

- It creates space for nervous system healing.

- It demands sovereignty.

Without separation, many twin flame unions would collapse under the weight of unintegrated wounds. Love pauses so wisdom can catch up. Separation is not failure. It is refinement.

Observing Without Absorbing

One of the most powerful lessons in this phase is learning to observe without absorbing. You can witness someone's fear without owning it. You can hold compassion without collapsing boundaries. You can love someone deeply and still walk away if the dynamic destabilizes you.

Empaths especially must learn:

You are not responsible for regulating another adult's emotional life. Sacred love does not require self-erasure. It requires self-trust.

TrueJoy Alchemy Pause

Place both feet on the ground.

Take a slow inhale.

Ask yourself:

Am I pursuing because I feel inspired — or because I feel afraid?

Let your body answer.

Your nervous system always knows before your mind does.

Ritual: Reclaiming the Flame

Light a candle.

Visualize your energy returning from every place you've overextended. See cords dissolving gently.

Whisper:

"I release the chase.
I release the fear.
I return to myself."

Place one hand on your heart.

Stay until your breath slows.

Reflection Prompts

- What does my body feel like when I want to chase?

- What am I afraid will happen if I stop reaching?

- What part of me believes love must be earned?

- Who am I without this connection?

Closing Mantra

I release urgency.
I choose sovereignty.
What is aligned meets me without pursuit.

Chapter 3

The Mirror Phase
Triggers, Projection & Emotional Alchemy

When the Mirror Stops Being Romantic At first, the mirror feels magical.

You see yourself reflected in someone's eyes and think,
"This is it. This is divine."

But eventually, the mirror stops flattering you. It starts revealing you. And that is where most people either awaken —
or blame.

The mirror phase is not the honeymoon.

It is the excavation.

What a Trigger Really Is

A trigger is not something someone "does to you."

A trigger is a stored emotional memory being activated in real time.

When your twin flame says something simple —
and your reaction feels disproportionate,
that is not coincidence.

It is memory meeting the present.

Twin flame connections intensify this because the mirroring is precise. They don't
just reflect your personality. They reflect your unfinished wounds.

If you fear abandonment, you will feel it intensely.
If you fear invisibility, you will feel overlooked.
If you fear control, you will react to pressure.

The connection does not create the wound.

It exposes it.

Projection: The Shadow We Assign to Another

Projection is one of the most powerful forces in relationships.

We unconsciously assign to another person the parts of ourselves we haven't
integrated.

For example:

If you suppress anger, you may accuse them of being aggressive.

If you suppress neediness, you may shame them for being dependent.

If you suppress ambition, you may feel intimidated by their drive.

Twin flame energy accelerates projection because it amplifies similarity. You
recognize yourself — but instead of integrating what you see, you externalize it.
Projection feels like certainty. But it is often unfinished self-recognition.

The Spiritual Bypass Trap

This phase is where spiritual language can become dangerous.

It is easy to say:

"They are triggering me because they are my twin."

It is harder to say:

"They are triggering me because there is something in me asking to be healed."

Spiritual bypassing happens when we use:

- "Divine timing"

- "Soul contracts"

- "Karmic clearing"

…to avoid taking responsibility for our emotional patterns.

Awakening is not about romanticizing dysfunction. It is about confronting it.
Divine love does not excuse unhealthy behavior. It illuminates it.

The Moment that I Saw Myself Clearly

There was a moment — quiet, humiliating, transformative —
when I realized I was reacting not to the present,
but to a ten-year-old version of myself.

The tone of voice.
The withdrawal.
The silence.

It wasn't him I was responding to. It was every moment in my childhood where
silence meant disapproval. That awareness did not make the pain disappear.

But it shifted the responsibility. Instead of demanding reassurance from him, I
began building safety within myself. That was the beginning of alchemy.

Emotional Alchemy: Turning Reaction into Wisdom

Alchemy is transformation.

In relationship work, it means:

Taking emotional activation
and turning it into awareness.

Instead of:

"You hurt me."

We ask:

"What did this activate in me?"

Instead of:

"You always leave."

We ask:

"What fear is surfacing right now?"

This does not excuse harmful behavior. It separates personal triggers from actual boundary violations. Mature love requires discernment between the two.

Clean Boundaries vs Trauma Defense

Not every reaction is projection. Sometimes a boundary is genuinely being crossed. The mirror phase requires brutal honesty.

Ask yourself:

Is my pain coming from:

- A current violation?

- Or a past wound?

If it is a current violation, address it directly. If it is a past wound, tend to it gently. Wisdom is knowing the difference.

The Power of Observing Without Absorbing

One of the most advanced relational skills is this:

Observing emotion without absorbing it.
You can witness someone's fear without becoming it.
You can hold space without collapsing into rescue mode.
You can feel love without merging identities.

Empaths struggle here most. Because mirroring feels like merging. But healthy mirroring is reflective — not absorptive. A clean mirror does not keep what it reflects. It reveals it and releases it.

When the Mirror Becomes Too Sharp

Sometimes the mirror reveals incompatibility. Sometimes what you see is not a wound to heal but a value mismatch to honor.

Not all twin flame connections are meant to last physically. Some are initiations. Some are awakenings. Some are seasons.

Clinging to a mirror after its lesson is complete creates stagnation. Letting go can be the highest form of integration.

The Real Work of the Mirror Phase

The mirror phase invites you to:

- Develop emotional literacy.

- Regulate your nervous system.

- Identify your attachment style.

- Integrate shadow traits.

- Strengthen boundaries.

- Separate fantasy from reality.

This is not romantic work. It is developmental work. And it is sacred. Because once you stop projecting, you start choosing consciously.

TrueJoy Alchemy Practice

Next time you feel triggered, pause.

Place your hand over your heart.

Ask:

What am I actually feeling?

Where have I felt this before?

What does this part of me need right now?

Respond to yourself before responding to them.

This is maturity.

Ritual: The Shadow Integration Exercise

Sit quietly with a journal.

Write the name of the person who triggers you.

Underneath, list three qualities about them that frustrate you.

Now ask:

Where does this trait exist in me — even subtly?

Write without censoring.

The goal is not shame.

It is integration.

When you integrate shadow, it loses power.

Reflection Prompts

- What patterns keep repeating in my relationships?

- What emotions do I struggle to tolerate?

- Where do I confuse chemistry with compatibility?

- What would it look like to respond instead of react?

Closing Mantra

I welcome the mirror.
I claim my shadow.
I transform reaction into wisdom.

Love refines me — it does not undo me.

Chapter 4

Self-Love as the First Sacred Union

Inner Masculine, Inner Feminine & Emotional Sovereignty

The Union You Were Actually Seeking

Every intense connection eventually brings you here.

To yourself.

After the recognition.
After the chase.
After the triggers.
After the collapse.

You stand alone and ask:

"What was I really searching for?"

And the answer — though humbling — is liberating.

You were searching for integration. Not another person. Not validation. Not destiny. Integration. The twin flame journey is less about finding someone to merge with and more about reconciling the split within yourself.

The Inner Split

Most of us grew up learning to suppress parts of ourselves.

Maybe you learned:

- To silence your needs to keep peace.

- To become hyper-independent to avoid disappointment.

- To over give to feel valuable.

- To detach to avoid vulnerability.

Over time, your internal energies fractured.

The intuitive, emotional self (inner feminine) may have felt unsafe.
The protective, structured self (inner masculine) may have become rigid or absent.

When these parts do not trust one another, you look externally for balance.

You seek someone to:

Hold you.
Ground you.
Validate you.
Stabilize you.
See you.

But if your inner feminine does not feel safe within your own boundaries,
no partner can permanently create that safety.

Inner Feminine: The Heart That Feels

Your inner feminine is not about gender.

It is about receptivity.

It is the part of you that:

Feels deeply.
Intuits quickly.

Creates naturally.
Softens when safe.
Yearns for connection.

When wounded, this energy can:

Over give.
Over attach.
Overidentify with relationship.
Lose itself in others' emotions.

The wounded feminine believes:

"If I love enough, I will be chosen."

But love is not something you earn.

It is something you embody.

Inner Masculine: The Structure That Holds

Your inner masculine is your boundary.

It is the part of you that:

Decides.
Protects.
Provides safety.
Maintains standards.
Holds vision.

When wounded, this energy can:

Withdraw.
Control.
Avoid intimacy.
Suppress emotion.
Shut down.

The wounded masculine believes:

"If I stay guarded, I will not be hurt."

But protection without openness becomes isolation.

The Sacred Marriage Within

True twin flame integration begins when these energies reconcile. When your inner masculine protects your inner feminine. When your inner feminine trusts your inner masculine.

When your heart feels safe because your boundaries are strong. When your softness is supported by discernment. This is inner union. This is the real sacred marriage.

And once this union is established internally, something profound shifts. You no longer pursue love out of urgency. You choose love out of resonance.

The Day I Stopped Needing to Be Chosen

There was a moment — quiet and almost invisible — when I realized something had changed.

I no longer needed him to validate my worth. I no longer felt frantic when he pulled away. I no longer interpreted silence as rejection.

It wasn't that I stopped caring. It was that I started containing myself. My inner masculine strengthened. My inner feminine relaxed. And the desperate edge dissolved.

That was the first time I understood what sovereignty actually feels like. It feels calm. It feels spacious. It feels like belonging to yourself.

Love as Frequency, Not Possession

When you are internally unified, love stops feeling like something to secure.

It becomes something to share.

You understand that:

God is Love.
The Universe is Love in motion.
You are an expression of that Love.

And love is not owned.
It is embodied.

When you live from love's frequency:

You don't chase.
You don't beg.
You don't overexplain.
You don't abandon yourself.

You align.

And alignment feels steady.

Why Self-Love Is Not Selfish

Many people fear self-love will make them less desirable. It does the opposite. Self-love creates coherence.

Coherence creates magnetism.

When your energy is stable, people feel it. When your boundaries are clear, respect follows. When you no longer tolerate inconsistency, inconsistency disappears.

Not because you control others. But because your nervous system no longer accepts dysregulation as love. Self-love filters chaos.

The Difference Between Independence & Sovereignty

Independence says:

"I don't need anyone."

Sovereignty says:

"I don't need to abandon myself for anyone."

Independence can be armor. Sovereignty is integration.

You can desire connection deeply and still remain sovereign. You can want partnership and still remain whole. The twin flame journey matures when desire no longer equals dependency.

Emotional Sovereignty

Emotional sovereignty means:

You are responsible for your reactions.
You regulate before responding.
You validate yourself before seeking validation.
You choose partners from peace, not panic.

This does not mean you never feel hurt.

It means you do not outsource healing.

When you stop asking others to rescue you from your own discomfort,
you become powerful. And power in love is quiet.

TrueJoy Integration Practice

Place one hand over your heart.
One hand over your lower belly.

Close your eyes.

Imagine your inner feminine standing before you — soft, feeling, open.

Now imagine your inner masculine standing beside her — steady, grounded,
protective.

Visualize them turning toward each other.

Not in conflict.
But in cooperation.

Say aloud:

"I honor my softness.
I honor my strength.
I trust myself to hold myself."

Stay until your breath slows.

Ritual: The Inner Covenant

Write a covenant to yourself.

It might begin:

"I will no longer abandon myself for love."

"I will not confuse chaos with chemistry."

"I will protect my peace."

Sign it.

Read it daily for seven days.

This is not affirmation.

This is agreement.

Reflection Prompts

- Where do I still abandon myself in relationships?
- What does my inner feminine need from me?
- What does my inner masculine need to strengthen?
- What standards am I ready to uphold?
- What would choosing from wholeness change?

Closing Mantra

I am whole.
I am sovereign.
I am the union I once sought.

Love flows through me —
not because I am chosen,
but because I remember who I am.

Part II — The Alchemy of Love
From Attachment to Alignment

Chapter 5

Attachment vs Alignment

Love, Limerence & the Nervous System

There is a difference between feeling drawn to someone
and being aligned with them. One feels urgent. The other feels steady.

One feels like you might lose something. The other feels like you are choosing something. Most confusion in modern love comes from misunderstanding this distinction.

We mistake activation for alignment. We mistake chemistry for compatibility. We mistake longing for love.

This chapter exists to restore clarity.

The Nervous System Is the Real Oracle

Before love becomes philosophy, it becomes biology. Every romantic connection activates your nervous system.

Your body scans for:

Safety
Familiarity
Threat
Belonging

And it does this long before your conscious mind forms an opinion. If someone feels familiar, your body reacts quickly. But familiarity does not automatically mean destiny.

Often, it means pattern recognition.

What Attachment Really Is

Attachment is not weakness. It is survival wiring. From infancy, your nervous system learned how to secure connection. If love was consistent, your system relaxed.

If love was unpredictable, your system adapted. If love was overwhelming, your system distanced. Those adaptations become adult attachment styles.

When a connection activates attachment patterns, it can feel cosmic. But what's often happening is this: Your body recognizes something it has experienced before. Not necessarily something healthy. Just something known.

Attachment says:
"If this leaves, I will lose stability."

Alignment says:
"If this stays, it supports who I am becoming."

Limerence: The Illusion of Destiny

Limerence is intense romantic infatuation combined with emotional dependency.

It feels like:

Obsessive thinking
Constant analysis
Mood swings based on contact
Idealization
Fear of rejection
Euphoria when reciprocated
Devastation when distant

Limerence floods the brain with dopamine. It activates the reward system in powerful ways. Intermittent attention strengthens it even more.

When someone is inconsistent, your nervous system becomes hyper-focused. The uncertainty fuels the attachment. This is not divine magnetism. It is reinforcement chemistry. Limerence feels like fate. But it is often anxiety seeking relief.

Attachment Activation Feels Like Love

Here's where many people get confused.

Attachment activation can feel spiritual.

You may think:

"This must mean something."

"It feels too strong to ignore."

"But I've never felt this before."

Intensity does not equal alignment. Intensity means your nervous system is highly engaged. Sometimes that engagement is attraction. Sometimes it is trauma memory. Often it is both. Without awareness, attachment masquerades as destiny. With awareness, attachment becomes information.

What Alignment Feels Like

Alignment is different. Alignment does not spike your nervous system. It steadies it.

You feel:

Calm curiosity
Mutual respect
Emotional safety
Room to breathe
Clear communication
Consistent effort

Alignment does not require guessing. You do not feel compelled to decode messages or interpret silence. There is clarity.

Alignment feels like expansion, not survival. You are not trying to secure the connection. You are participating in it.

The Body Test

If you remove the fantasy and listen only to your body, you will know.

Attachment feels like:

Tight chest
Racing thoughts
Sleep disruption
Compulsive checking
Emotional swings

Alignment feels like:

Open breath
Stable mood
Clear thinking
Comfortable silence
Ease after interaction

This does not mean alignment is boring. It means it is regulated. And regulated love is sustainable love.

Divine Chemistry vs Trauma Chemistry

There is such a thing as divine chemistry. But divine chemistry does not destabilize you long-term. It may awaken you. It may challenge you. It may expand you.

But it will not chronically dysregulate you. Trauma chemistry feels intoxicating. Divine chemistry feels grounding.

Trauma chemistry asks:
"Will they stay?"

Divine chemistry asks:
"Are we building something real?"

One creates obsession. The other creates devotion.

Why We Confuse the Two

If your early love experience included unpredictability, your body learned to equate tension with connection. Calm can initially feel unfamiliar. You may even interpret steadiness as lack of passion.

But often what feels "boring" is actually safety. And safety is the soil where deep passion grows over time. Adrenaline fades. Stability compounds.

From Attachment to Alignment

The shift from attachment to alignment begins with one question:

"Do I feel powerful here — or dependent?"

Attachment feels like:

"I need this to work."

Alignment feels like:

"I choose this if it works."

Attachment is outcome-driven. Alignment is value-driven. Attachment negotiates self-respect. Alignment protects it.

Reclaiming Power

When you understand your nervous system, you reclaim authority.

You stop asking:

"Why do I feel so pulled?"

And start asking:

"What is this activating in me?"

You stop chasing reassurance. You build regulation. You stop romanticizing intensity. You value coherence.

This is where power returns. Not power over another person. Power over your participation.

Secure Love Is Built, Not Found

Secure love is not lightning. It is architecture.

It is built through:

Consistency
Transparency
Repair after conflict
Mutual responsibility
Shared vision

Secure love is not dramatic. It is deliberate. It feels peaceful. And peace is powerful.

TrueJoy Integration Practice

Close your eyes.

Take five slow breaths.

Think of someone you feel strongly about.

Now ask:

Do I feel steadier — or more anxious — when I imagine building with this person?

Let your body answer.

Your nervous system always reveals truth.

Reflection Prompts

When have I mistaken intensity for alignment?

How does my body respond to uncertainty in love?

What does safety feel like physically?

Where do I still chase reassurance?

Am I willing to choose calm over chemistry?

Closing Mantra

I release love that activates fear.

I choose love that supports growth.

I trust steadiness more than urgency.

I align before I attach.

Chapter 6

The Stages of Awakening
From Projection to Presence

Love does not evolve in a straight line.

It unfolds in layers.

At first, it feels like recognition.
Then intensity.
Then confusion.
Then collapse.
Then clarity.

What most people call the "twin flame journey" is not about relationship destiny. It is about consciousness development. It is the process of moving from projection to presence.

From fantasy to embodiment. From emotional dependency to emotional sovereignty. This chapter maps that evolution in grounded terms.

Stage One — Recognition

The Mirror Appears

Recognition feels electric. You meet someone and something inside you wakes up.

You feel seen.
Activated.
Understood.
Exposed.

It can feel ancient. But recognition is not completion. It is amplification. What you are recognizing is not your missing half. You are recognizing parts of yourself reflected back with intensity.

Desire.
Wounds.
Power.
Fear.
Potential.

The mirror appears — and it is bright. This stage teaches you: You are capable of deep connection. But it does not yet teach you stability.

Stage Two — Projection

Seeing Through Fantasy

After recognition, projection begins. You assign meaning. You build narrative. You interpret signs.

You may think:

"This is destiny."
"This is different."
"This must last."

Projection is not foolish. It is human. When something feels significant, the mind tries to anchor it. But projection often overlays unmet needs onto another person.

The anxious projects salvation. The avoidant projects engulfment. The wounded projects rescue. The lonely projects permanence.

Projection feels romantic. But it is unfinished integration. This stage teaches you:

You must separate what is real from what is imagined.

Stage Three — Activation

When the Shadow Surfaces

Intensity reveals shadow. This is where the nervous system becomes loud. Old abandonment wounds surface.

Fear of loss intensifies. Jealousy appears. Control patterns emerge.

You may think:

"They changed."

But often, what changed is your illusion. Activation is not punishment. It is exposure.

The connection magnifies what has not yet healed. And now you are faced with a choice:

React from fear
or
Respond from awareness

This stage teaches you:

Emotional maturity cannot be bypassed.

Stage Four — Separation

The Sovereignty Test

Separation is misunderstood. It is often labeled failure. But in truth, separation is a nervous system reset. When intensity exceeds capacity, distance creates integration space.

Separation may look like:

Silence
Withdrawal
Physical distance
Emotional detachment
Life redirection

It feels painful because attachment is activated. But separation asks a powerful question:

Who are you without this story?

This stage forces identity reconstruction.

If your sense of self was wrapped around the connection, separation reveals that dependency. This is not loss. It is initiation.

This stage teaches you: You must become whole whether they stay or go.

Stage Five — Surrender

Releasing the Outcome

Surrender is not passivity. It is power. It is the moment you stop negotiating your peace.

You stop analyzing messages. You stop interpreting every silence. You stop trying to control timing.

You say:

"If this is aligned, it will meet me in clarity.
If it is not, I will still be steady."

Surrender shifts energy. Not because you manipulated it. But because you reclaimed it.

This stage teaches you:

Peace is not dependent on reunion.

Stage Six — Integration

Becoming Regulated

Integration is quieter than activation. There are no fireworks here. There is regulation.

Your nervous system stabilizes. You sleep better. You think clearly. You stop obsessing. You feel less reactive.

You may still care. But you no longer feel destabilized. This is where true growth happens.

You understand:

The connection was the catalyst.
The work was yours.

Integration teaches you: Wholeness is internal.

Stage Seven — Conscious Union (If It Occurs)

Not every journey ends in physical reunion. And that is not failure. But when reunion happens after integration, it feels different.

There is no urgency. No chasing. No power struggle.

Conversations feel grounded. Boundaries feel respected. Effort is mutual.

You are not trying to secure love. You are building it. If conscious union does not occur externally, something even more important has.

You have become internally secure. And secure love meets secure people.

This stage teaches you:

Love is not possession.
It is participation.

The Real Evolution

This journey dismantles illusion.

It exposes:

Romantic fantasy
Attachment dependency
Emotional immaturity
Identity collapse in relationships

And it rebuilds:

Self-trust
Regulation
Discernment
Boundaries
Alignment

This is not mystical destiny. It is developmental maturity. And maturity is spiritual.

The Grounded Reality Check

Not every intense connection follows all these stages. Sometimes it is simply incompatibility. Sometimes it is a karmic loop.

Sometimes it is chemistry without coherence. The stage model is not meant to romanticize suffering. It is meant to bring clarity to growth.

If a connection does not lead toward sovereignty, it is not evolving. Growth is the metric. Not reunion.

TrueJoy Integration Practice

Sit quietly.

Take three slow breaths.

Ask:

What stage am I truly in?

Not the romantic answer.

The honest one.

Now ask:

What is this stage asking me to strengthen?

Identity?
Boundaries?
Regulation?
Self-trust?

Growth accelerates when fantasy dissolves.

Reflection Prompts

Where have I confused intensity with evolution?

What did separation teach me about myself?

What illusion has dissolved through this experience?

If reunion never happens, what have I gained?

What does mature love require from me now?

Closing Mantra

I honor every stage of awakening.

I release fantasy.

I choose growth over attachment.

I build love from wholeness.

Chapter 7

Discernment in Love

Soulmates, Karmic Partners & Sacred Mirrors

Not every powerful connection is meant to stay. Not every intense connection is sacred. Not every calm connection is ordinary.

Spiritual maturity in love begins when you stop asking,
"Who are they to me?"
and start asking,
"Who am I becoming in this?"

Discernment is not cynicism. It is clarity. And clarity protects your heart.

The Temptation to Label

When a connection feels significant, we want language for it.

Twin flame.
Soulmate.
Karmic partner.
Divine counterpart.

Labels give meaning. But meaning can quickly turn into attachment. When we label too quickly, we often stop evaluating honestly.

We cling to the title instead of assessing the behavior. The truth is simpler: The label matters less than the lesson. The relationship is sacred only if it moves you toward integrity.

Karmic Connections

Lessons Wrapped in Chemistry Karmic relationships are often magnetic. They feel familiar immediately. But the familiarity is usually pattern recognition.

These connections tend to:

Activate attachment wounds
Repeat emotional cycles
Feel addictive
Create dramatic highs and lows
End abruptly or painfully

Karmic love is not punishment. It is repetition. It exposes what remains unintegrated.

But here is the key:

If the pattern repeats without growth, the lesson has stalled.

Staying too long in karmic loops becomes self-abandonment. Karmic connections teach through friction. Once the lesson integrates, the pull weakens.

Soulmate Connections

Harmonized Alignment Soulmates feel different. There is depth — but without chaos. There is familiarity — but without fear. There is attraction — but without urgency.

Soulmate relationships often feel like:

Calm support
Shared values
Mutual effort
Natural flow
Emotional safety

You feel more yourself — not less. Soulmates can be romantic partners. They can also be friends, mentors, children, collaborators.

They stabilize rather than destabilize. Soulmate love does not burn wildly. It builds steadily. And steady love creates longevity.

Sacred Mirrors

Catalysts of Awakening Some connections act as accelerators. They ignite rapid growth.

They expose shadow quickly. They destabilize illusion. These are sacred mirrors.

They are not necessarily meant to last forever. They are meant to wake you up. Sacred mirrors often involve:

Intense activation
Rapid transformation
Identity shifts
Emotional exposure

But here is the distinction:

Sacred mirrors lead to sovereignty.

Karmic loops lead to repetition.

If a connection expands your self-trust, it is awakening you. If it erodes your stability, it is repeating you. Growth is the metric. Not intensity.

The Body Never Lies

Discernment begins in the nervous system.

Before labeling a connection, ask:

Do I feel regulated here?

Do I feel respected here?

Do I feel safe expressing truth?

Does my body soften or tighten?

Love that requires constant recovery is not alignment. Love that feels like peace is not boring. It is mature.

The Danger of Romanticizing Intensity

In modern culture, we have glorified emotional chaos. We call it passion. We call it depth. We call it destiny.

But chronic anxiety is not romance. Emotional instability is not spiritual awakening. Inconsistency is not mystery.

If you feel smaller, confused, or perpetually unsure, something is misaligned. Sacred love does not require suffering to prove itself. It invites expansion without self-loss.

When Spiritual Language Becomes Avoidance

Spiritual terminology can become a shield against reality.

"It's divine timing."
"It's karmic clearing."
"We have a soul contract."

Perhaps.

But discernment asks:

Are we accountable?
Are we respectful?
Are we evolving?

Spiritual maturity increases responsibility.

It does not excuse immaturity.

If love destabilizes your nervous system repeatedly without repair, that is not sacred design. It is misalignment.

The Evolution Question

Instead of asking:

"Are they my soulmate?"

Ask:

"Do we grow well together?"

Instead of asking:

"Is this destiny?"

Ask:

"Is this healthy?"

Instead of asking:

"Will this last forever?"

Ask:

"Does this reflect my integrity?"

The most evolved love is not dramatic.

It is aligned.

Expanding Beyond One Person

One of the greatest spiritual shifts happens when love expands beyond romantic fixation.

You begin to recognize sacred connection in:

Friendship
Collaboration
Mentorship
Community

You realize that love is not concentrated in one individual. It is an ecosystem. And when you widen your focus, obsession dissolves. Belonging deepens. Your world grows.

Choosing From Wholeness

Discernment is not about rejecting connection. It is about choosing from sovereignty. When you are whole, you no longer chase intensity.

You choose resonance. You no longer romanticize suffering. You require stability.

You no longer cling to labels. You look at behavior. And behavior reveals alignment more clearly than words ever will.

TrueJoy Discernment Practice

Think of a connection that feels significant.

Now ask yourself:

Am I more peaceful or more anxious in this relationship?

Am I expanding or shrinking?

Am I building something stable or surviving something unstable?

Write the answers honestly.

Your nervous system is your compass.

Trust it.

Reflection Prompts

Where have I used labels to avoid clarity?

What connection in my past was karmic — and what did it teach me?

What does secure love feel like physically?

Where do I still equate intensity with importance?

What standards am I now ready to uphold?

Closing Mantra

I choose clarity over fantasy.

I choose growth over repetition.

I choose peace over chaos.

I choose love that honors my wholeness.

Chapter 8
Sacred Reciprocity
Boundaries, Clean Giving & Emotional Maturity

Love cannot thrive without reciprocity. Not intensity. Not destiny. Not chemistry. Reciprocity.

Sacred love is not built on longing. It is built on mutual participation. On two regulated individuals choosing to give and receive without collapse.

This chapter is where romantic fantasy gives way to relational maturity. Because love that is not reciprocal will always feel unstable. And instability is not sacred.

The Difference Between Giving and Over-giving

Many spiritually inclined people pride themselves on generosity. They give. They support. They forgive. They understand. But generosity without boundaries becomes depletion.

Over-giving often looks like:
Making excuses for inconsistency
Carrying emotional weight alone
Initiating every repair
Minimizing your own needs
Staying quiet to keep peace

Over-giving is not love. It is fear of loss. Sacred love does not require self-erasure. It requires self-respect.

Clean Giving

Clean giving comes from wholeness.
It sounds like:
"I choose to give this."
Not:
"I give so you won't leave."

Clean giving has no hidden contract. It does not expect repayment. It does not resent effort. It does not manipulate.

Clean giving is powerful because it comes from sovereignty. When two people give cleanly, love becomes light. When one person over gives, love becomes heavy.

The Courage to Receive

Reciprocity is not about giving only. It is about receiving. Many people struggle more with receiving than giving.

Receiving requires vulnerability. It requires believing you are worthy of care. It requires relaxing control.

Some people give endlessly because it feels safer than receiving. But love cannot flow in one direction. If you cannot receive, intimacy will remain incomplete. Sacred love flows both ways.

Emotional Responsibility

Reciprocal love depends on emotional responsibility. Each person must regulate themselves before engaging the other.

This means:
Owning reactions
Apologizing when wrong
Communicating clearly

Respecting boundaries
Repairing after conflict

You are not responsible for regulating another adult's emotional life. You are responsible for how you show up. Mature love feels calm because both nervous systems carry themselves.

Boundaries as Devotion

Boundaries are often misunderstood as rejection. But boundaries are devotion to integrity.

A boundary says:
"I value this connection enough to protect its health."

Without boundaries:
Resentment grows.
Confusion builds.
Imbalance festers.

With boundaries:
Clarity increases.
Trust strengthens.
Safety deepens.

Sacred reciprocity requires clear lines. Not rigid walls. Not porous merging. Clear lines.

The Test of Mutual Effort

Here is a simple question:

If you stopped initiating, would the connection continue?
If the answer is no, you are not in reciprocity.

You are in pursuit.

Love that must be chased is not aligned. Love that meets you willingly builds itself. Mutual effort does not require constant intensity. It requires consistency. Consistency is romantic in its own way. It builds trust.

Stability Is Not Boring

Many people unconsciously equate stability with lack of passion. But instability is exhausting. And exhaustion erodes intimacy.

Sacred reciprocity feels:
Predictable in effort
Respectful in communication
Transparent in intention
Honest in limitation

It may not feel like fireworks every day. But it feels safe. And safety allows depth.

Speaking Life Into Each Other

Mature love does not relate only to wounds. It sees potential. It affirms growth. It invokes evolution.

You see the king or queen in the other. Not to idolize them. But to encourage alignment.

You speak:
"You are capable."
"I see your strength."
"I trust your growth."

Sacred partnership calls each other higher without controlling each other.
This is not chasing.
This is honoring.

When Reciprocity Is Missing

If you consistently feel:
Uncertain
Unchosen
Unseen
Unheard
Unvalued

Pause.
Do not spiritualize imbalance. Do not romanticize effort disparity. Do not label instability as destiny.

Reciprocity is not a luxury. It is the minimum requirement for sustainable love. Without it, connection becomes negotiation. With it, connection becomes collaboration.

Sacred Reciprocity in Practice

Reciprocity looks like:
Both initiate.
Both apologize.
Both express needs.
Both adjust.
Both choose.

No one is carrying the relationship alone. No one is convincing the other to stay. No one is performing worthiness.

Two sovereign people meet in mutual commitment. That is sacred.

The Freedom of Balanced Love
When love becomes reciprocal, something relaxes. You stop scanning for signs. You stop overanalyzing silence. You stop overcompensating.

You trust the structure. You trust the rhythm. And when trust is present, intimacy deepens naturally. Peace replaces urgency.

TrueJoy Integration Practice

Think of your current or most recent relationship.

Ask yourself:
Where was I giving cleanly?
Where was I over-giving?
Where did I struggle to receive?
Where was reciprocity present?

Write the answers without judgment.
Clarity restores power.

Reflection Prompts

What does balanced effort look like to me?
Do I confuse over-giving with devotion?
How do I respond when my needs are unmet?
What boundaries strengthen my integrity?
What would reciprocal love change in my life?

Closing Mantra

I give from wholeness.
I receive with openness.
I choose mutual effort.
I build love that is balanced.

Transition to Part III
From Personal Healing to Collective Love

There comes a moment in every awakening when love stops being about one person. It stops being about reunion. It stops being about longing. It stops being about deciphering signs.

It becomes something quieter. More powerful. It becomes about how you live. When attachment settles and discernment sharpens, something profound shifts.

You are no longer asking:
"Who is meant for me?"
You are asking:
"What am I meant to build?"

This is the natural evolution of mature love.

When the Nervous System Stabilizes

Once your nervous system is regulated, your focus expands.
You stop orbiting a single connection.

You begin investing in:
Friendship
Community
Collaboration
Purpose
Family
Legacy

Love becomes less concentrated and more distributed. Not diluted. Expanded. The obsession dissolves. The clarity remains. And from clarity, contribution emerges.

Love as Ecosystem

In early awakening, love feels like lightning. In maturity, love feels like architecture.

You understand now that:
No one person is responsible for your sense of belonging.
Belonging is built through many aligned relationships.

The heart was never meant to anchor to one flame alone. It was meant to light a network. This is where personal healing becomes collective healing.

The Shift From Chemistry to Contribution

At first, you are consumed by chemistry. Then you seek alignment.

Now you are ready for something deeper:
Contribution.

How does your love improve the emotional field around you?
How does your regulation impact your family?
How does your integrity shift generational patterns?
How does your presence calm rooms?

Mature love asks not just:
"Who completes me?"

But:
"How does my wholeness serve others?"
This is where love becomes legacy.

Expanding the Definition of Sacred Connection

When you are no longer fixated on romantic resolution, you begin to see sacred connection everywhere. In the friend who understands you without explanation. In the mentor who challenges you to grow. In the child who softens your defenses. In the community that reflects your values.

Sacred love is not rare. It is relational maturity expressed in many forms. The twin flame archetype may have awakened you.

But now you are awake. And awakened love does not limit itself to one person. It widens.

The Calm After the Storm

If you feel less reactive now…
Less desperate…
Less preoccupied…
That is not loss.
That is integration.

Peace is not the absence of passion. It is the presence of stability. And stability creates space for something extraordinary: Purposeful connection.

Entering Part III

Part III is not about romance.
It is about resonance.

It explores:
Soul family
Collective healing
Sacred partnership as service
Love that builds beyond personal fulfillment
You are no longer searching.
You are shaping.
You are no longer asking for rescue.
You are becoming a steady presence.

This is where love matures into leadership.
Quietly.
Naturally.
Grounded.
Let's widen the lens.

Part III — Love Beyond Romance
Expanding Into Collective Love

Chapter 9

The Reunion Within
When Love Becomes a State, Not a Person

For many, the word reunion carries hope. It suggests return.
A message.
A conversation.
A reconciliation.
A restored relationship.

But true reunion is not about someone coming back. It is about you coming home.
There is a moment in every awakening when longing softens. Not because the
story resolved.

But because you did.

The Illusion of External Completion

When love feels intense, we often attach peace to outcome.

"I'll feel whole when they choose me."
"I'll relax when we're together."
"I'll understand everything when we reunite."
But this keeps completion outside of you.

It makes peace conditional. And conditional peace is fragile. The connection may
have awakened something powerful. But it was never designed to complete you.

It was designed to reveal you.

What Reunion Within Actually Feels Like

Reunion within does not feel dramatic. It feels steady.

It feels like:
Sleeping through the night.
Thinking clearly again.
Not checking your phone compulsively.
Not replaying conversations.
Not interpreting silence.
It feels like emotional space.

You still care. But you are not destabilized. You are no longer trying to secure something. You are secure.

The End of Urgency

Urgency is attachment's language.
Reunion is calm.

Attachment says:
"I need resolution."
Reunion says:
"I have clarity."

Attachment seeks proof. Reunion trusts alignment. You may still think of them.

But the thoughts are neutral. The charge is gone. And without the charge, obsession dissolves. This is not indifference.

It is integration.

The Nervous System Shift

When you stop chasing outcome, your nervous system recalibrates.
Cortisol lowers.
Sleep improves.
Appetite stabilizes.
Identity strengthens.
Your body no longer lives in hypervigilance.

This is not mystical. It is biological healing. You stop scanning for signs. You start living your life. And that is reunion.

When Physical Reunion Happens

Sometimes physical reunion does occur. But if it happens after internal reunion, it feels different. There is no desperation.

No bargaining. No power imbalance. There is conversation. Clarity. Mutual effort.

If the connection cannot meet you at your new level of stability, you walk away calmly. Because you are no longer afraid of being alone. That is power. And power does not chase.

If Physical Reunion Never Happens

Then something even more profound has.
You have reunited with yourself.

You have integrated:
Your attachment wounds.
Your fear of abandonment.
Your longing for validation.
Your need for control.
You have reclaimed your center.

And once you return to center, you cannot be destabilized the same way again. Reunion was never about them. It was about you remembering who you are without them.

Reunion With Source

Beyond psychology, there is something deeper. When longing collapses, space opens. In that space, you reconnect with something greater than relationship.

You reconnect with Love itself. Not romantic love. Not conditional love.

But the quiet awareness that:
God is Love.
The Universe moves in coherence.
And you are not separate from that movement.

This awareness does not feel euphoric. It feels grounded. You feel held — not by a person, but by reality itself. That is sacred.

The Day the Waiting Ended

There is a subtle moment when waiting stops. It does not announce itself.

You wake up and notice:
You are thinking about your day.
Not about the story.
You are planning your future.
Not imagining reconciliation.
You are building.
Not pausing.

That is the quietest and most powerful transformation. You are no longer waiting to be chosen. You are choosing your life.

The Shift From Longing to Leadership

Longing is inward. Leadership is outward. When reunion integrates, your energy expands.

You invest in:
Friendships.
Creative projects.
Family.
Community.
Purpose.
You stop orbiting one connection.
You begin shaping your world.

This is where love matures into contribution.

The Freedom of Wholeness

Wholeness does not mean you never desire partnership. It means your desire does not destabilize you. You can want love deeply. And still remain steady.

You can open your heart. And still protect your boundaries. You can choose partnership. Without losing yourself. Reunion within is the foundation for every secure relationship that follows.

TrueJoy Integration Practice

Sit comfortably.
Place one hand on your heart.
Take five slow breaths.
Whisper:
"I am already whole."
"I release urgency."
"I trust alignment."
Stay until your body softens.
Notice the difference between longing and belonging.

Reflection Prompts

Where have I postponed peace waiting for outcome?
What has this connection taught me about myself?
What does emotional steadiness feel like now?
If reunion never happens, what have I gained?
What am I ready to build from wholeness?

Closing Mantra

I release the search.
I return to center.
I build from clarity.
I am whole.
And from wholeness, love meets me.

Chapter 10

Soul Family & Collective Healing
When Love Expands Beyond the One

There is a natural shift that happens after reunion within. The intensity that once revolved around one person begins to soften. Your energy stabilizes. Your attention widens.

And something subtle but powerful occurs: You begin to notice how many forms love actually takes. You realize the story was never about one flame.

It was about awakening your capacity to love consciously. And conscious love does not isolate. It expands.

The Myth of "The Only One"

When we are attached, we narrow love into a single figure.

We believe:
"They are my person."
"They are my destiny."
"They are the only one who understands me."

But when emotional integration happens, a new truth emerges:
There are many aligned connections in a lifetime.
Not identical.
Not interchangeable.
But meaningful.
Soul family is not about exclusivity.

It is about resonance.

What Soul Family Actually Is

Soul family is not mystical hierarchy. It is relational alignment.

It is the experience of meeting someone and feeling:
Ease.
Clarity.
Shared values.
Mutual growth.

There is no destabilizing intensity. No power struggle. No emotional volatility disguised as passion. There is steadiness.

Soul family feels like:
"I don't have to perform here."
You are seen without needing to prove yourself.
And you offer the same in return.

The Nervous System Knows

When a connection is aligned, your body tells you.
Your breath slows.
Your posture softens.
Your thoughts become coherent.
You do not feel pulled.
You feel grounded.

After intense attachment experiences, this steadiness may feel unfamiliar at first. You might even mistake it for "boring." But it is not boring. It is safe. And safety is the soil where real intimacy grows.

From Romantic Obsession to Relational Ecosystem

Mature love understands something important:
No one person can meet every emotional need.
Healthy adults build ecosystems.
Friends for laughter.
Mentors for growth.
Partners for intimacy.

Community for belonging.
Family for history.
Colleagues for purpose.

When love becomes distributed across aligned relationships, pressure reduces. And pressure reduction prevents collapse. This is collective healing.

Breaking the Cycle of Emotional Dependency

Many of us were conditioned to believe:
If one relationship fails, everything fails.
If one person leaves, we are abandoned.

But emotional maturity teaches something different:
Loss does not erase worth.
Separation does not erase belonging.
One connection does not define your future.
When you stop concentrating your identity in one person, you stabilize your life.
And stability creates resilience.

Generational Healing

When you shift from attachment to alignment, you interrupt patterns.

You stop reenacting:
Anxious pursuit.
Emotional withdrawal.
Over-functioning.
Under-communicating.
People-pleasing.
Emotional volatility.

You become the regulated nervous system in the room. And regulated systems change families. Children raised around steadiness develop differently.

Partners exposed to emotional maturity evolve differently. Friends learn safety through example. Healing is not dramatic. It is behavioral. And behavior changes lineage.

Leadership Without Ego

At this stage, love is no longer about proving anything. You are not trying to be spiritually advanced. You are not trying to demonstrate awakening.

You are simply living in coherence. You speak directly. You choose carefully. You walk away calmly.

You invest intentionally. Leadership here is quiet. It is not loud declarations of destiny. It is consistent integrity.

Community Over Fantasy

Fantasy isolates. Community stabilizes.

Fantasy says:
"One person will change my life."
Community says:
"We support each other's growth."

When you move into collective love, you stop searching for the singular hero narrative. You build mutual strength instead. And this reduces emotional volatility.

The Calm Expansion

Notice what has changed:
You are no longer scanning for signs.
You are not decoding silence.
You are not replaying old conversations.

You are:
Planning.
Collaborating.
Creating.
Connecting.
Living.

The obsession is gone. The clarity remains. And from clarity, contribution emerges.

TrueJoy Integration Practice

Sit comfortably.
Take three steady breaths.
Ask yourself:
"Where am I concentrating too much emotional energy?"
"Where can I expand my support system?"
"Who in my life feels safe, steady, and reciprocal?"
Write down three names.
Reach out to one this week.
Healing is relational.
Not theoretical.

Reflection Prompts

What patterns did I inherit that I am no longer repeating?
What does healthy community feel like in my body?
Where do I still romanticize intensity over stability?
How can I strengthen my ecosystem of support?
What kind of emotional field do I create in a room?

Closing Mantra

I do not concentrate my worth in one connection.
I build alignment in many.
I create steadiness around me.
I become the regulated presence I once searched for.

Chapter 11

Sacred Union & Shared Purpose

When Two Whole People Build Together

By the time you reach sacred union, something fundamental has changed. You are no longer looking to be saved. You are no longer trying to prove your worth through devotion. You are no longer chasing intensity to feel alive.

You are steady.

And from steadiness, you can finally choose clearly. Sacred union is not about finding "the one." It is about recognizing alignment between two regulated, self-aware adults.

Union Is Not Completion

Completion is an illusion born from insecurity.

Healthy partnership is not: "You complete me."
It is: "I am whole. You are whole. Let's build."

When two people come together from wholeness, the dynamic shifts dramatically. There is no performance. No rescuing. No fixing. No emotional bargaining. There is clarity.

What Sacred Union Actually Looks Like

It looks surprisingly ordinary.
• Calm conversations.
• Repair after conflict.
• Accountability without collapse.
• Boundaries without punishment.
• Emotional transparency without oversharing.
• Sexual intimacy rooted in trust, not validation.
• Shared goals grounded in reality.

It feels stable. And stability, after chaos, can feel unfamiliar. But unfamiliar does not mean wrong. It means regulated.

The Nervous System Match

Sacred union requires nervous system compatibility. If one person is chronically dysregulated and the other is not, imbalance forms. If one person avoids conflict and the other pursues it aggressively, volatility forms.

Sacred union is not about chemistry alone.
It is about co-regulation.
Do you both calm each other?
Do you both take responsibility?
Do you both repair after rupture?
Do you both invest equally?
If the answer is yes, you are building something sustainable.

The Shift From "Meant To Be" to "Mutually Chosen"

Early attachment says:
"This was meant to be."
Mature love says:
"We are choosing this."

Choice creates power. Destiny removes responsibility. Sacred union is not fated.

It is maintained. Every day. Through behavior. Through communication. Through alignment.

Shared Purpose Without Ego Inflation

Purpose in partnership is not:
"We are here to change the world."
It is:
"We live in a way that improves the world around us."

That might mean:
Raising emotionally secure children.
Building ethical businesses.
Creating stable homes.
Supporting community.
Serving with integrity.
Living honestly.
Shared purpose does not require global recognition.

It requires coherence. If your relationship makes you more grounded, more honest, more responsible, more kind — it is serving purpose.

Power Without Control

Sacred union holds power carefully.
No manipulation.
No silent treatment.
No scorekeeping.
No leveraging vulnerability.

Instead:
Direct requests.
Clear boundaries.
Repair after mistakes.
Mutual growth.
Power becomes constructive.
Not defensive.

Seeing the Sovereign in Each Other

Mature love does not shrink partners. It expands them. You speak to their potential without controlling it.

You encourage growth without forcing it. You support autonomy without fearing loss. You want them to thrive — even if it requires change.

This is the difference between attachment and devotion. Attachment grips. Devotion supports.

Conflict in Sacred Union

Conflict does not disappear. It matures. In sacred union:

Disagreement is information. Triggering moments are opportunities. Silence is not punishment.

Distance is not threat. Both partners stay. Not because they are afraid to leave. But because repair matters.

When Sacred Union Is Not Aligned

Sometimes two healthy people are simply not aligned. Sacred union does not require suffering to prove love.

If values differ significantly. If growth directions oppose each other. If long-term vision conflicts.

Walking away calmly can be sacred too. Union is not endurance. It is coherence.

The Legacy of a Regulated Partnership

The most powerful partnerships are not dramatic. They are stable. And stability changes environments.

Children raised in regulation develop differently. Teams led by emotionally mature couples function differently. Communities influenced by coherent partnership grow differently. Sacred union becomes legacy not through intensity — but through consistency.

TrueJoy Integration Practice

Sit quietly and reflect:
Does this relationship make me more stable or more anxious?
Do I feel safe to express truth?
Do we repair conflict effectively?
Are we aligned in long-term direction?
If you are single:
What kind of nervous system do I want to co-regulate with?
What behaviors define stability for me?
What standards am I now clear about?
Write your answers.
Clarity prevents future confusion.

Reflection Prompts

What does "choosing" love look like in action?
Where have I mistaken chemistry for compatibility?
How do I show up in conflict?
Am I building something, or just experiencing something?
What does partnership at its healthiest look like in daily life?

Closing Mantra

I choose alignment over intensity.
I choose steadiness over urgency.
I choose partnership that builds.
I build love with clarity.
And I walk away from what destabilizes me.

Part IV — Embodiment
Living the Love You Discovered

Chapter 12

Rituals for Conscious Relationships

Turning Insight Into Daily Practice

By now, you understand something essential:
Love is not a feeling you sustain.
It is a practice you maintain.
The strongest relationships are not the most romantic.
They are the most regulated.
They are built on small, repeated behaviors that protect trust.
Rituals are not grand gestures.
They are consistent anchors.

Why Rituals Matter

When relationships fail, it is rarely because of one dramatic moment. It is because of slow drift. Unspoken resentment. Unrepaired conflict. Unexpressed appreciation.

Assumed understanding. Avoided conversations. Ritual interrupts drift. It creates structure for connection. Not intensity.

Stability.

Daily Ritual: The Three-Minute Reset

This can be done in partnership or alone.
At the end of the day, ask:
• What did I appreciate about you today?
• Is there anything unresolved?
• Is there anything I need tomorrow?
No debate.
No overanalysis.
No emotional excavation.
Just clarity.
Small repair prevents large fracture.

Weekly Ritual: Alignment Check

Set aside one uninterrupted hour.
Ask each other:
• Where are we aligned right now?
• Where do we need adjustment?
• What does each of us need this week?
• Are we protecting our energy?
No phones.
No multitasking.
Consistency matters more than depth.
Regular maintenance reduces crisis.

The Nervous System Pause
Before difficult conversations:
Pause.
Take five slow breaths.
Place both feet on the floor.
Lower your tone intentionally.
Regulated conversations prevent escalation.

If either partner is dysregulated:
Delay the conversation.
You do not repair from survival mode.

Appreciation as Protection

Many relationships collapse from neglect, not betrayal. Appreciation is
protective. Say thank you for ordinary things.

Notice effort. Acknowledge growth. Reinforce stability. Respect grows through
recognition.

Boundaries Without Drama

Conscious relationships require boundaries.
Not walls.
Not punishment.
Not silent treatment.

Clear statements:
"I'm not available for that."
"I need space to think."
"I'm feeling overwhelmed."
"That doesn't work for me."

Calm boundaries increase safety. Explosive reactions reduce it.

Conflict as Curriculum

Conflict is inevitable. How you handle it defines maturity.

Avoid:
Character attacks.
Historical stacking.
Threats.
Withdrawal as control.

Practice:
Owning your part.
Listening fully.
Stating needs clearly.
Repairing quickly.

The goal is not to win. It is to restore stability.

Sexual Intimacy as Grounded Connection

Conscious intimacy is not performance-based. It is not validation-driven. It is not urgency-fueled.

It is:
Mutual.
Communicated.
Safe.
Present.
When emotional safety increases, intimacy deepens naturally.
Without emotional safety, intensity replaces connection.

The "Are We Growing?" Conversation
Every few months, ask:
• Are we evolving?
• Are we supporting each other's growth?
• Is our life expanding or shrinking?
• Are we still choosing this?

Growth must be mutual. If only one person is evolving, imbalance forms. Sacred union requires movement.

Ritual for Singles: Preparing the Field
If you are not currently partnered:
Your rituals still matter.

Daily:
• Protect your energy.
• Strengthen friendships.
• Invest in purpose.
• Practice boundaries.
• Regulate your nervous system.

You do not prepare for love by longing. You prepare by stabilizing. Aligned partnership meets stable energy.

The Simplicity of Conscious Love

There is no secret technique. No mystical code. No cosmic sign required.

Healthy relationships are built on:
Honesty.
Regulation.
Consistency.
Repair.
Choice.
Repeat.
Over and over.

TrueJoy Practice: The Integrity Scan

Once a week, ask yourself:
Did I communicate clearly?
Did I abandon myself anywhere?
Did I over-function?
Did I withdraw instead of repair?
Did I choose alignment over ego?
Self-awareness strengthens partnership.

Reflection Prompts

What rituals would protect my current relationship?
Where does drift occur most often?
What makes me feel emotionally safe?
How do I contribute to safety for others?
What behaviors will I no longer tolerate?

Closing Mantra

Love is not maintained by intensity.
It is maintained by integrity.
I choose clarity.
I choose repair.
I choose steadiness.
I build love through action.

Chapter 13

Living as Love

Identity, Integrity, and Emotional Coherence

At some point, the conversation about love stops being about relationships.
It becomes about who you are.
Not who you attract.
Not who you lost.
Not who you reunited with.
But who you are when no one is watching.
This is where the journey matures.

Love as Identity
Early in life, love feels external.
Something you receive.
Something you chase.
Something you lose.

But as you grow, something shifts. Love becomes internal. It becomes how you speak. How you choose. How you regulate. How you respond under pressure.

It becomes identity. Living as love does not mean being agreeable. It means being coherent.

Your thoughts align with your words.
Your words align with your actions.
Your actions align with your values.
This is emotional integrity.

Coherence Over Performance

Many people perform love. They use soft language while holding resentment. They appear calm while suppressing truth. They preach awareness while avoiding accountability.

Coherence is different.

Coherence is:
Saying what you mean.
Meaning what you say.
Following through consistently.
It is not loud.
It is not dramatic.
It is reliable.
Reliability is love in motion.

Emotional Leadership

When you become regulated, you influence rooms without trying. You become the steady presence in chaos. Not because you suppress emotion — but because you process it.

Emotional leadership means:
You do not escalate unnecessarily.
You do not personalize everything.

You do not abandon yourself to keep peace.
You do not chase validation.
You respond instead of react.
That alone changes environment.

Breaking Cycles Quietly

You may never receive applause for your healing. No ceremony. No public acknowledgment.

But cycles break quietly.
When you choose not to yell.
When you choose not to chase.
When you choose not to manipulate.
When you choose to walk away calmly.
When you choose repair instead of pride.
You alter your lineage.

This is generational healing. Not through intensity. Through consistency.

Boundaries as Self-Respect
Living as love includes limits.

It includes:
Saying no.
Ending conversations.
Leaving misaligned spaces.
Reducing exposure to chaos.
Refusing emotional games.
This is not coldness.
It is clarity.
Love without boundaries becomes resentment.
Love with boundaries becomes strength.

The End of Romantic Obsession

When love becomes identity, obsession dissolves.
You no longer romanticize instability.
You no longer confuse longing with depth.
You no longer chase unavailable people to prove your worth.
You recognize compatibility faster.
You leave misalignment sooner.
You invest more wisely.
This is empowerment.
Not detachment.
Discernment.

Integrity in Ordinary Moments

Living as love is not about spiritual declarations.

It is about:
Returning phone calls.
Keeping commitments.
Admitting mistakes.
Apologizing sincerely.
Managing your tone.
Listening fully.
Leaving when needed.
It is ordinary.
And powerful.

Self-Trust as the Final Integration

The most profound shift of this journey is self-trust.
You trust:
Your nervous system.
Your instincts.
Your boundaries.
Your standards.
Your timing.
You no longer need constant reassurance.
You do not require constant confirmation.
You choose from clarity.
And clarity simplifies life.

Love in Leadership, Work, and Community

When you live as love, it extends beyond partnership.
You lead differently.
You parent differently.
You negotiate differently.
You collaborate differently.
You become less reactive.
More direct.
More consistent.
More honest.

This builds reputation. Reputation builds influence. Influence builds legacy.

The Steady Flame

The twin flame story began with intensity.
But it ends with steadiness.
The steady flame does not flicker wildly.
It warms.
It lights.
It sustains.
And it does not depend on another person to stay lit.

TrueJoy Integration Practice

Once a week, ask:
Where was I reactive?
Where was I regulated?
Where did I abandon myself?
Where did I stand firm?
Where did I act from clarity instead of fear?
Write it down.
Growth is measured through awareness.

Reflection Prompts

What does living as love look like in my daily behavior?
Where do I still seek validation?
What are my non-negotiable standards now?
How do I handle conflict differently than I once did?
What kind of emotional environment do I create for others?

Closing Mantra

I am not searching for love.
I am living it.
I do not perform love.
I embody it.
I choose clarity.
I choose integrity.
I choose steadiness.
And from that place,
everything aligns.

Chapter 14

Becoming the Light
Embodiment, Integrity, and the Legacy of Love

At the beginning of this journey, love felt like something that happened to you.
It felt sudden.
Intense.
Destabilizing.
Transformative.
Now it feels different.
It feels chosen.
Steady.
Clear.
Intentional.
That shift is everything.
You are no longer reacting to love.
You are embodying it.

The Difference Between Awakening and Embodiment

Awakening is dramatic.
Embodiment is consistent.
Awakening feels like lightning.
Embodiment feels like architecture.
One reveals.
The other builds.

Many people awaken.
Few integrate.

Integration is quieter. It is showing up the same way on hard days as you do on easy ones. It is maintaining boundaries even when loneliness tempts you to abandon them. It is speaking truth even when silence would be easier.
That is becoming the light.

Light Without Performance

Becoming the light is not about appearing enlightened. It is not about spiritual language. Not about aesthetic calm. Not about curated peace.

It is about internal coherence. Your values match your behavior. Your standards remain intact under pressure.

Your responses reflect regulation, not impulse. You do not need others to witness your growth for it to be real. Private integrity is the strongest form of light.

The Legacy of Regulated Love

Intensity leaves stories.
Regulation leaves stability.
Stability leaves legacy.
When you live from clarity:
Children feel safer.
Partners feel respected.
Teams function better.
Communities strengthen.
Conflicts resolve faster.
You reduce chaos simply by refusing to contribute to it.

That is influence. And influence compounds over time.

Walking Away Without Drama

One of the clearest signs of embodiment is how you leave.
No speeches.
No emotional manipulation.
No scorched earth.
Just clarity.
"This does not align."
"This no longer feels healthy."
"This is not sustainable."
Then you go.
Without revenge.
Without obsession.
Without collapse.
That is power.

Building Instead of Reacting

Reactive love asks:
"How do I keep this?"
Embodied love asks:
"What am I building?"

You build:
A life.
A home.
A network.
A body of work.
A reputation.
A lineage of emotional maturity.
You stop pouring energy into emotional loops.
You redirect it toward structure.
And structure stabilizes identity.

Responsibility as Strength

Becoming the light means accepting responsibility for:
Your triggers.
Your communication.
Your boundaries.
Your patterns.
Your growth.

Not because you are to blame for everything. But because ownership increases power. Blame keeps you stuck. Ownership moves you forward.

The End of Romantic Illusion

You no longer romanticize chaos.
You no longer label instability as fate.
You no longer confuse emotional volatility with depth.

You recognize quickly:
Safe feels calm.
Aligned feels steady.
Healthy feels reciprocal.
And you do not apologize for wanting peace.
Peace is not settling.
It is clarity.

What Remains

After all the awakening, separation, reunion, discernment, partnership, and expansion —
What remains is simple.
Self-trust.
You trust your pace.
Your standards.
Your nervous system.
Your discernment.

You do not rush love.
You do not chase clarity.
You do not tolerate misalignment.
You move deliberately.

That is embodiment.

Love as Contribution

At its highest form, love is not about romance.
It is about contribution.
How do you contribute to:
Stability?
Safety?
Honesty?
Repair?
Clarity?
Growth?

You become someone who reduces harm.

Someone who communicates directly.
Someone who apologizes when necessary.
Someone who leaves when appropriate.
Someone who builds instead of breaks.

That is light.

The Steady Flame Revisited

The twin flame story began with fire. But this is a different flame. This one does not scorch.

It sustains.
It warms.
It lights your path without blinding you.
It does not require intensity to prove it exists.
It simply burns.

And it does not depend on anyone else to remain lit.

TrueJoy Integration Practice

Sit quietly.
Place both feet on the floor.
Take five slow breaths.
Ask yourself:
What am I building now?
Where am I still reacting instead of choosing?
Where do I need firmer boundaries?
Where am I proud of my growth?
Write the answers.
Then choose one small action that reflects embodiment this week.
Light is built through behavior.

Reflection Prompts

How has my definition of love matured?
What standards do I now hold consistently?
What patterns have I permanently ended?
Where do I still need refinement?
What kind of emotional legacy am I creating?

Closing Mantra

I do not chase love.
I cultivate it.
I do not perform light.
I live it.
I choose integrity.
I choose clarity.
I choose steadiness.
And through that steadiness,
I become the light.

Epilogue — Love Without End

There is no final chapter to love. There are only new expressions. Every ending in your life has simply been love changing form.

A relationship ending.
A story dissolving.
A version of you falling away.

Love was never leaving. It was evolving. You will meet yourself again and again.

Through partnership.
Through solitude.
Through joy.
Through grief.

Each time, you will remember:

You were never separate.
You were never incomplete.
You were always home.

Love does not end. It refines. Walk gently. Love boldly.

Let your life be your ceremony.

A Note from Joy

Beloved,

If these pages found you in heartbreak, I hope they leave you in clarity. If they found you in longing, I hope they leave you in sovereignty. If they found you chasing a person, I hope they leave you choosing yourself.

This book was born from lived experience.

From confusion.
From awakening.
From humility.
From growth.

I do not write as someone who escaped love's lessons. I write as someone who integrated them. TrueJoy Living exists because I learned that joy is not found in another person.

It is cultivated within. And from that place, sacred partnership becomes possible.

Wherever you are in your journey, know this:

You are not behind.

You are becoming.

With reverence,

Joy Hafner
Founder, TrueJoy Living

Final Blessing

Love Is What You Are

May you never again confuse intensity with destiny.

May you choose stability over chaos.

May your heart remain open,
but never unprotected.

May you walk in self-respect.

May your love build, not burn.

May your presence calm rooms.

May your relationships be reciprocal.

May your healing ripple through generations.

May you remember, especially in quiet moments:

God is Love.
The Universe is Love in motion.
And you are an expression of that Love.

Love is not something you find.

It is what you are.

And so it is.

Reader Reflection Pages

What I Know Now

Take time with these. Write honestly. This is the moment integration becomes real.

What did I believe about love before reading this book?

What do I believe about love now?

What patterns have I recognized in myself?

Where have I mistaken intensity for alignment?

What does secure love feel like in my body?

What boundaries am I now committed to keeping?

How will I embody love differently going forward?

What legacy do I want my relationships to leave?

Who am I becoming?

Close your journal.

Place your hand over your heart.

Whisper:

"I know now.
I am whole.
I choose love with clarity."

And begin again.